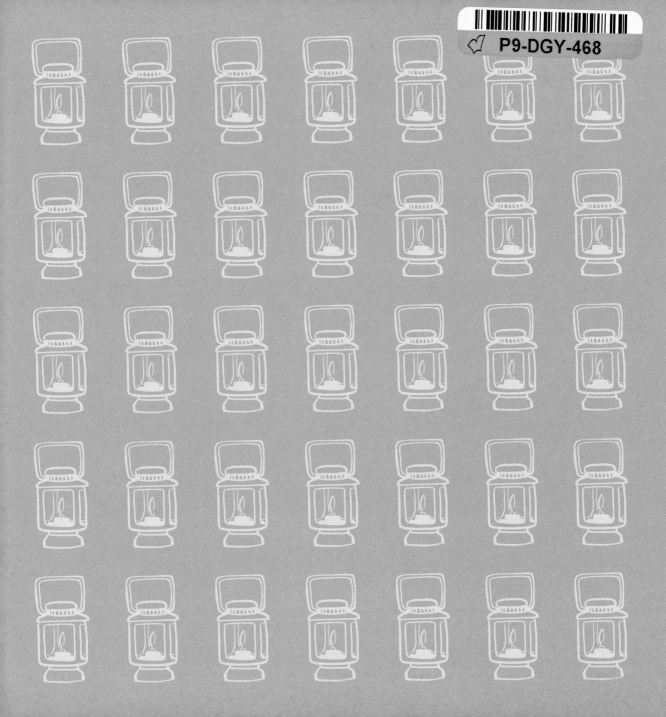

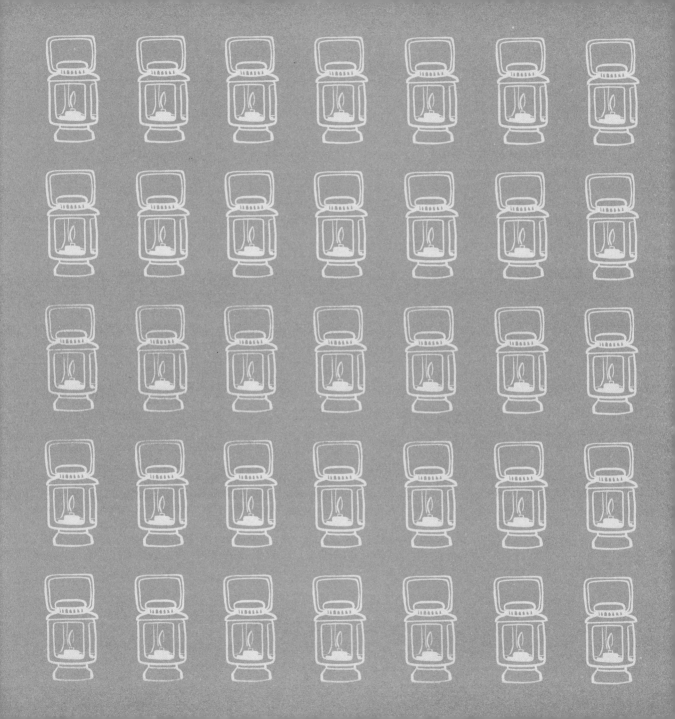

ORDINARY
PEOPLE
CHANGE
the
WORLD

I am Harriet Tubman

BRAD MELTZER

illustrated by Christopher Eliopoulos

 DIAL BOOKS FOR YOUNG READERS

I am **Harriet Tubman.**

Do you know what the North Star is?
It's one of the brightest stars in the sky.
Unlike other stars, which may seem to move,
the North Star always stays where it is.
When you find it, it'll show you which way is north.

Back when I was growing up, in certain parts of the country,
if you were black, you were most likely enslaved.
We didn't have a choice.
Being enslaved meant we were forced to work without pay.
We were treated terribly.

We lived in tiny shacks with no windows.
We slept on the floor, or in boxes filled with straw.
As kids, we had to wear sacks.
And they certainly didn't celebrate our birthdays,
or keep records of when we were born.

The next time they came, though, my mother was ready.
Someone wanted to buy my younger brother.
She had asked other slaves to help her hide my brother
in the woods—*for nearly a month!*
But eventually, they found him.

It was a powerful moment: my mother standing up to those men.
Was it dangerous? Definitely.
But it was right.
After that, they didn't sell my brother.

As early as I can remember, I loved listening to my mother tell stories.
She taught me some of life's most important lessons.
Being enslaved, it was against the law for us to read or write.
But she told me stories from the Bible, including the tale of...

When I was around six years old, it was my turn to start working. I still lived with my family, but my owners hired me out to another farm.

What would happen if we didn't do what they said?
Our owners would whip us, or worse.

But by hearing my story, I hope you'll find strength you never knew you had.

That's what happened when I was around seven years old.

I was working in my owner's house and went to grab a lump of sugar from a nearby bowl.

I'D NEVER TASTED SUGAR BEFORE.

IT LOOKED SO GOOD.

HOW DARE YOU TOUCH MY SUGAR?!

She reached for something to hit me with. I ran as fast as I could.

When I got to someone else's farm, I hid in their pigpen. That's how scared I was.

For five days, I stayed there, hiding in the mud, fighting

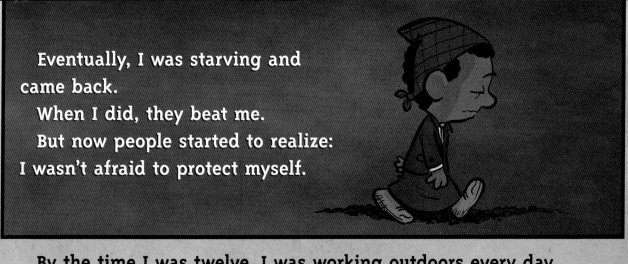

Eventually, I was starving and came back.
When I did, they beat me.
But now people started to realize: I wasn't afraid to protect myself.

By the time I was twelve, I was working outdoors every day, where the hardest work was done.
I hoed, harvested, and lifted heavy barrels of flour.
I got so strong and was chopping so much wood, even the men could barely keep up.

Working in the fields gave me more than physical strength.

It gave me time to learn from other enslaved people.

Time to consider new ideas.

During that time, I spent many nights looking at the sky.
My father was the one who taught me about the North Star.

It hit me instead.
Hard.

I got knocked out.

It was an injury
that forever changed
my life.
Since I didn't die,
I decided God had a
plan for me, and was
guiding and protecting
me.

After my injury, I started having vivid dreams.
I'd be flying like a bird over fields and towns, over rivers and mountains.
In the air, I'd reach a great fence—and on the other side would be a
big, beautiful field.

But each time, no matter how hard
I tried, I could never get over that line.

My brothers and I planned to escape, but they got scared and turned back. So I went all by myself. I traveled by night, following the North Star—just like my father had taught me.

THIS IS THE WAY.

IT'LL **ALWAYS** LEAD ME RIGHT.

I stayed in the houses of people who wanted to help us find freedom.

THERE ARE **SLAVEHUNTERS** ALL OVER.

WEAR THESE MEN'S CLOTHES SO NO ONE WILL RECOGNIZE YOU.

YOU'RE SAVING MY LIFE.

I was now traveling on what was called the Underground Railroad.

It wasn't a real railroad; it didn't have tracks or train cars. And it didn't go underground. It was people who didn't like slavery secretly helping people escaping from slavery.

But it did have special stations: safe hiding places run by black and white helpers we called conductors.

It even had its own signals.

THE PASSWORD FOR THE NEXT SAFEHOUSE IS A HOOT SOUND, LIKE AN OWL.

USE THAT AND THEY'LL GIVE YOU A PLACE TO SLEEP.

THANK YOU FOR PROTECTING ME.

On the Underground Railroad, we were safe.

On my next trip back to Maryland, I helped free my youngest brother, whose name was Moses, as well as two other men.

THE WAY YOU'RE LEADING PEOPLE TO FREEDOM...

YOU SURE *I'M* THE ONE WHO SHOULD BE CALLED *MOSES?*

AFTER THAT, I MADE ANOTHER RESCUE TRIP. AND *ANOTHER.*

I RESCUED FAMILY AND FRIENDS.

On the Underground Railroad, we used hiding places like attics, potato cellars, and barns. Some folks even built secret tunnels and hidden rooms, like this fake closet.

IN HERE.

YOU'LL BE SAFE.

C'MON... FOLLOW ME.

I also continued wearing disguises.

WHY ARE YOU DRESSED LIKE AN OLD LADY?

SO NO ONE WILL RECOGNIZE ME.

PUT THIS ON.

WE'RE GONNA GET YOU OUT OF HERE.

FOLLOW ME.

THAT WOMAN...

SHE'S SAVING OUR LIVES.

With each trip, our Underground Railroad helped more slaves escape.

Soon, they started calling me the "Moses" of my people.

To stay out of sight, I traveled by night, sticking to the backroads.

I also made many of my trips in the winter, when people wouldn't be outside their homes.

Occasionally, it was so hard to walk over the mountain passes, even the bigger and supposedly stronger men would want to stop.

I always kept them going, leading the way.

On this particular night, we ran out of money.

But I was so committed to keeping everyone safe that I gave away some of my own clothing, including my underwear, to pay for the place where we slept.

On another trip to buy some live chickens, I spotted one of my old masters—someone I used to work for when I was enslaved!

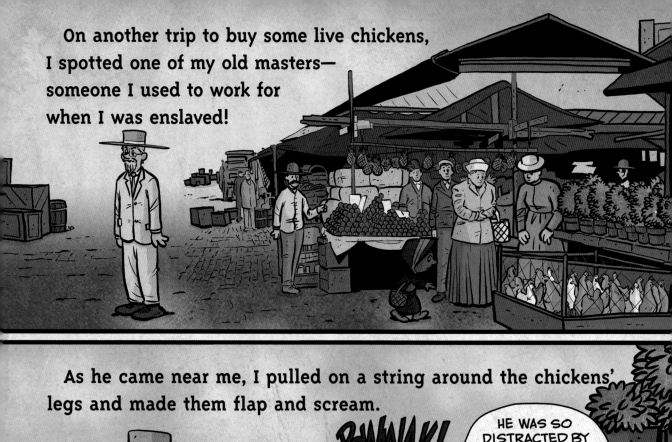

As he came near me, I pulled on a string around the chickens' legs and made them flap and scream.

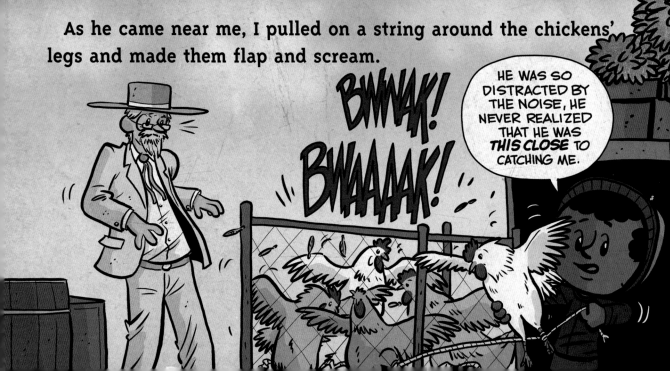

BWWWAK!

BWAAAAK!

HE WAS SO DISTRACTED BY THE NOISE, HE NEVER REALIZED THAT HE WAS *THIS CLOSE* TO CATCHING ME.

Over eleven years, I went back to Maryland thirteen times, personally freeing around seventy people.

To keep them safe, I led many of them to Canada, which is where I brought five of my siblings, my niece, and even my own parents.

The more I fought against slavery, the more
I realized that the only way to win...

...was to end slavery itself.
That chance came as the Civil War began.

THE **NORTHERN** PART OF THE COUNTRY WANTS TO **STOP** SLAVERY.

THE **SOUTH** WANTS TO **KEEP** IT.

AT FIRST, I TOOK CARE OF WOUNDED SOLDIERS. BUT SOON, MY BEST TALENTS WERE PUT TO USE.

This is Secretary of War Edwin Stanton.

LOOK AT THIS INFORMATION SHE HAS COLLECTED. HARRIET TUBMAN AND HER SPY RING ARE REMARKABLE.

Soon after, I became the first American woman ever to lead an armed raid into enemy territory.

With the information we found, we successfully fought the Southern soldiers.

Most important, we proved that Black people could serve in the military just as well as white people.

Eventually, the North won the Civil War and slavery ended.
But that didn't mean my battles were over.
I became a community activist, then traveled around
the country, talking about injustice.

After the war, I was so poor, I had to burn pieces of my
fence for firewood.
But as always, I kept battling, helping those who needed it.

When I was nearly ninety years old, my dream of helping others grew even bigger as I established a new home in Auburn, New York, for poor, old, and sick African Americans.

In my life, I was told I couldn't make my own choices.
Told I would never escape.
But I did.
I fought for my independence.
And once I had breathed the air of freedom,
I knew I needed to help others breathe it too.

The measure of success isn't what you achieve for yourself, it's what you do for others.

Think of yourself as a bird.

Some days, you'll climb high; some days, you'll fall.

But when you pass the clouds and reach the top, you have a choice:

You can stay up there and enjoy the view—or you can go back down...

In every life, we face hard decisions.
At those times, we can make the safe choice...
or the right choice.
Would you put yourself at risk to help someone else?
Would you stand up to someone mighty in order to
help someone who is weak?

To answer those questions, you must follow your heart—your own North Star.
It will always point you in the right direction.

I am Harriet Tubman.
Follow me.
I will lead the way to freedom.

"I was the conductor of the Underground Railroad for eight years, and I can say what most conductors can't say—I never ran my train off the track and I never lost a passenger." —Harriet Tubman

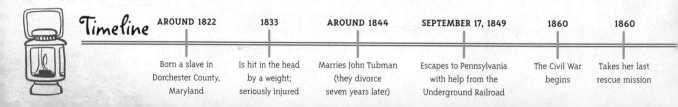

Timeline

AROUND 1822	1833	AROUND 1844	SEPTEMBER 17, 1849	1860	1860
Born a slave in Dorchester County, Maryland	Is hit in the head by a weight; seriously injured	Marries John Tubman (they divorce seven years later)	Escapes to Pennsylvania with help from the Underground Railroad	The Civil War begins	Takes her last rescue mission

Harriet (far left) next to her adopted daughter, Gertie, and her husband, Nelson, among others, 1887

Plaque at Harriet's birthplace in Maryland

HARRIET TUBMAN
1820-1913

THE "MOSES OF HER PEOPLE," HARRIET TUBMAN OF THE BUCKTOWN DISTRICT FOUND FREEDOM FOR HERSELF AND SOME THREE HUNDRED OTHER SLAVES WHOM SHE LED NORTH. IN THE CIVIL WAR SHE SERVED THE UNION ARMY AS A NURSE, SCOUT AND SPY.

MARYLAND CIVIL WAR CENTENNIAL COMMISSION

Memorial statue in Harlem, New York City

JANUARY 1, 1863	1863	1865	1869	JUNE 23, 1908	MARCH 10, 1913	APRIL 20, 2016
President Lincoln's Emancipation Proclamation frees all U.S. slaves	Becomes first woman to lead a military raid	The Civil War ends	Marries Nelson Davis	Harriet Tubman Home for the Aged officially opens	Dies in Auburn, New York	U.S. Treasury announces future twenty-dollar bill with Harriet's face on the front

For Bari,
my sister,
one of the strongest people I know,
and who reminds me of the power of family
—B.M.

For Mike Jung, who got me through
high school and life by showing me the world
of comics and graphic storytelling
—C.E.

For historical accuracy, we used Harriet Tubman's actual dialogue whenever possible. For more of her true voice,
we recommend and acknowledge *Harriet Tubman: The Life and the Life Stories* by Jean M. Humez and
Bound for the Promised Land: Harriet Tubman, Portrait of an American Hero by Kate Clifford Larson.
Special thanks to Jean M. Humez and Bacardi Jackson for their input on early drafts.

· ·

SOURCES
Harriet Tubman: The Life and the Life Stories by Jean M. Humez (University of Wisconsin Press, 2004)
Bound for the Promised Land: Harriet Tubman, Portrait of an American Hero by Kate Clifford Larson (Ballantine Books, 2003)
Harriet Tubman: The Road to Freedom by Catherine Clinton (Little, Brown, 2004)
Harriet Tubman: The Moses of Her People by Sarah Bradford (Dover Publications, 2004)
"Harriet: The Modern Moses of Heroism and Visions" by Emma P. Telford (Cayuga County Museum, 1905)
Heroine in Ebony by Robert W. Taylor (George H. Ellis, 1901)

FURTHER READING FOR KIDS
Minty: A Story of Young Harriet Tubman by Alan Schroeder (Dial Books for Young Readers, 1996)
Moses: When Harriet Tubman Led Her People to Freedom by Carole Boston Weatherford (Hyperion, 2006)
Who Was Harriet Tubman? by Yona Zeldis McDonough (Grosset & Dunlap, 2002)

· ·

DIAL BOOKS FOR YOUNG READERS
Penguin Young Readers Group · An imprint of Penguin Random House LLC · 375 Hudson Street, New York, NY 10014

Text copyright © 2018 by Forty-four Steps, Inc. · Illustrations copyright © 2018 by Christopher Eliopoulos

ISBN 9780735228719

Photo of Harriet Tubman on page 38 courtesy of Swann Auction Galleries; page 39 photo of the historical marker from
The Washington Post courtesy of Getty Images; page 39 photo of the statue by Jim Henderson, Wikimedia Commons.

Printed in China · 10 9 8 7 6 5 4 3 2 1
Designed by Jason Henry · Text set in Triplex · The artwork for this book was created digitally.

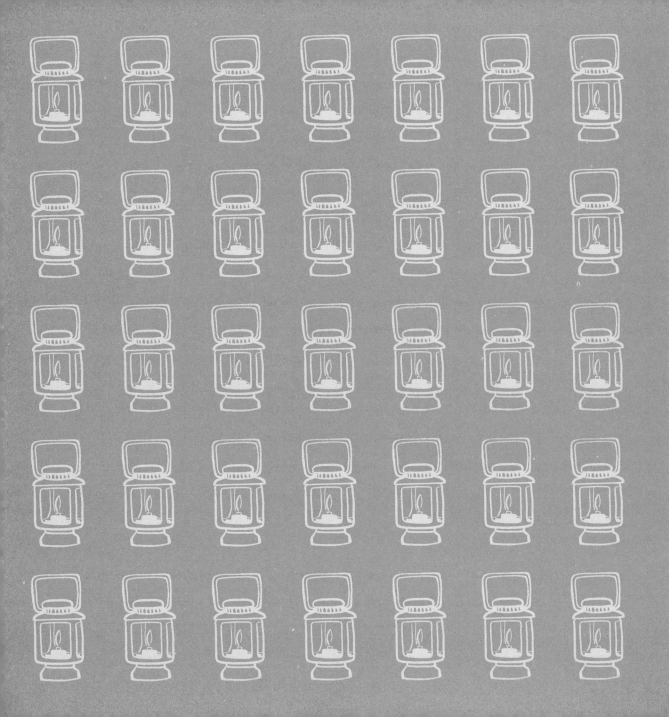